IMAGES
of America

LOUISIANA'S
OIL HERITAGE

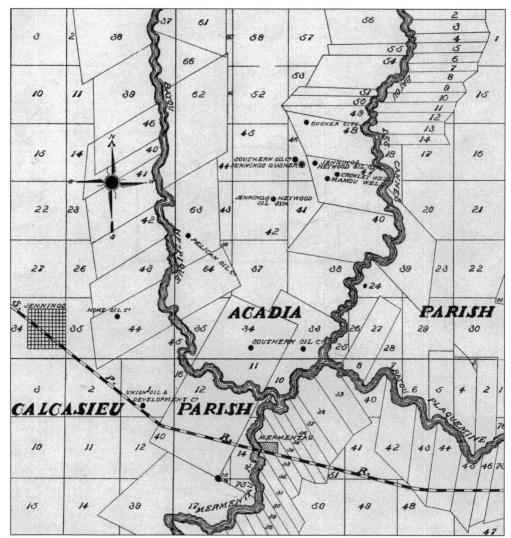

In 1902, the Louisiana oil industry was in its first year. A map of the Jennings Oilfield showed just 10 wells in the Mamou Prairie between Bayou Nezpique and Bayou des Cannes. Railroads and pipelines did not yet exist in the Jennings and Evangeline Fields, and the Ford Model T automobile had not yet been invented, but Louisiana was already producing thousands of barrels of oil each day. Louisiana recently celebrated its 110th year in the oil industry. Given the abundance of petroleum resources in the state and off its shore, Louisiana will have many more years to celebrate its oil culture and heritage. (Jennings Carnegie Public Library.)

ON THE COVER: In 1912, the Caddo Field in northwest Louisiana was in its heyday, and everyone was drilling for oil. The first offshore well had just been drilled in Caddo Lake the year before, and pipelines were being laid to connect the field to refineries throughout the area. Fred Stoval, a driller from north Louisiana, brought in this well with his crew on November 24, 1912. (State Library of Louisiana.)

IMAGES
of America

LOUISIANA'S OIL HERITAGE

Tonja Koob Marking and Jennifer Snape

ARCADIA
PUBLISHING

Published by Arcadia Publishing
Charleston, South Carolina

Library of Congress Control Number: 2012938384

For all general information, please contact Arcadia Publishing:
Telephone 843-853-2070
Fax 843-853-0044
E-mail sales@arcadiapublishing.com
For customer service and orders:
Toll-Free 1-888-313-2665

Visit us on the Internet at www.arcadiapublishing.com

To Travis, for supporting my horizontalism. To my grandfather Jay, with whom I would have loved to share this book.

CONTENTS

ACKNOWLEDGMENTS

Institutions and libraries across Louisiana graciously opened their archives to share with us their precious holdings of Louisiana's oil heritage for inclusion in this book. Harriet Shultz of the Jennings Carnegie Public Library gave us full access to its collections of the first oilfield in Louisiana; Pati Threatt pulled countless boxes off the McNeese State Library shelves for us to hunt and gather photographs of the southwestern fields; Coe McKenzie at the Oil City Museum grabbed photographs from museum exhibits of the Caddo and Pine Island Fields for us to scan and include in this collection. Everyone at Louisiana State University in Shreveport was very helpful with scanning images and providing historic information. Florence Jumonville at the University of New Orleans had an extensive knowledge of its collections that helped us find what we needed. Virgil Allen of the International Petroleum Museum & Exposition provided photographs of *Mr. Charlie* and took us on a tour of the historic rig. Without their help, this book would not be possible, and we sincerely thank them for indulging our insatiable desire for vintage oilfield images.

We also want to thank Simone Monet-Williams, our editor at Arcadia Publishing, for her enthusiastic support of our project. Her excitement made us believe that our wild idea of writing a book to share our love of vintage oilfield photographs with the people of Louisiana could and would become a reality. We also thank Laura Snape for her work formatting the hundreds of images we gathered for this project. Her organization of our documents made writing this book much easier than if we had had to figure out the imaging software on our own.

Finally, to my husband, Travis, thank you for walking with me along the circuitous paths of my varied and endless interests.

—Tonja

To my family and Josh, thank you for allowing me to take time out of our vacations for writing and researching and for supporting my ambitions.

—Jenny

INTRODUCTION

Louisiana's culture and heritage are world renowned for their unique regions and flavors. People from Louisiana are easily recognized by their accents, their attitudes, and their traditions. For Louisianans, their roles and their ancestors' roles in the development of the petroleum industry are a continuing source of pride. Louisiana was home to many firsts in the oil industry, including the first offshore oil well and the first interstate natural gas pipeline, and that pride of discovery and invention is still evident today in its citizens and towns throughout the state.

Louisiana's oil heritage began in Jennings on September 21, 1901, when W. Scott Heywood brought in the first successful oil well on the Mamou Prairie of Acadiana. Oil fever spread north to Caddo Lake and Pine Island, south to Hackberry, Cameron, and Morgan City, east to Terrebonne and Lafourche, and offshore to the Gulf of Mexico. Louisiana had a new industry that provided work opportunities and wealth to its citizens on a scale that had not previously existed in the state's agrarian-based economy. Men who had worked as subsistence farmers could now seek those opportunities to provide better lives for their children. Families moved to the oil patch, and parents raised their children in oilfield camps and educated them in oilfield school tents.

Oil and gas extraction has historically been important to Louisiana, not only for the deposits and associated petroleum-related activities but also for its close proximity to exploration and production facilities in the Gulf of Mexico. From the onset of oil exploration along the coast in the 1920s, petroleum development brought additional wealth to Louisiana and profoundly affected the lives and the thinking of its inhabitants. Oil-related companies brought an influx of "out-of-towners" to Louisiana who in turn spawned the development of service-related businesses, including restaurants, motels, and washaterias, to support the oil-business workers. Literally thousands of people were employed in the exploration or production of oil and gas. Thousands more worked for service companies necessary for the proper operation of the petroleum industry, including trucking, oilfield supplies, refining, and distribution.

Fifty years after the discovery of oil in Louisiana, the state held a golden jubilee in Jennings on September 21, 1951, to honor the "old timers" and their achievements in the petroleum industry. To continue honoring that industrious culture, beginning in the early 1950s, every October, Louisiana celebrated Oil Progress Week. Local newspapers would dedicate an entire section to articles and advertisements honoring the petroleum industry. Local, regional, and national companies and organizations showed their support through advertisements and contributed articles during Oil Progress Week. Mud Supply Company, Inc., announced it was "proud of the achievements of the Oil Industry . . . glad that we play such a vital role in those spots where Oil is BORN in Louisiana!" W.T. Burton proclaimed "In Petroleum's Progress Lies FUTURE" in a full-page advertisement. Non-oil companies like Powell Lumber purchased half-page advertisements showing their involvement in the petroleum industry. Farm Supply and Awning Company proclaimed in its advertisement, "Oil increases production on the Farm Front," including a drawing of a farm complete with windmill. Even Gordon's Drug Stores announced "Oil . . . Prescription for Progress" and "Medicines and Pharmaceuticals Out of an Oil-Well."

In 1951, Cit-Con Oil Corporation's and the Evangeline Refining Company's advertisements appeared alongside the headline of an article that read "Petroleum Industry Is Most Democratic, Attracts Men From All Walks of Life." On the opposite page, Humble Oil & Refining Company declared, "The people of Louisiana know the story well: as home folks in the oil country, they share the oil industry's pride in supplying the resource that powers a major share of the country's industries, all its airplanes and automobiles, most of its ships and trains." It continued regarding the value of crude oil produced in Louisiana, "This is not 'boom money.' Louisiana uses it to pay taxes, salaries and wages; it buys homes, groceries, light and heat; doctors collect a portion of it; landowners receive royalty and lease payments; a sizable portion of it is reinvested in the further development of the state's oil resources."

Women involved in the petroleum industry also celebrated their roles during Oil Progress Week. The Desk and Derrick Club announced its newly organized association and board members in the October 21, 1951, issue of the *Lake Charles American Press*. The Desk and Derrick Club was "formed to give the working women of oil companies and associated firms a better understanding of the oil industry." Nationally, the club had over 1,500 members, and the local organization planned "a program of talks by industry executives, field trips to refineries, wells, and research laboratories, and other activities covering the entire industry."

Local communities continue the celebrations honoring the oil and gas industry with annual festivals. Cameron hosts the Fur and Wildlife Festival, Morgan City has the Shrimp and Petroleum Festival, and Caddo sponsors Gusher Days. Museums honoring Louisiana's oil heritage are the Louisiana State Oil and Gas Museum in Oil City and the International Petroleum Museum & Exposition in Morgan City.

Louisiana's oil heritage celebrated its 110th year on September 21, 2011. This book documents its first 60 years with 196 vintage images. It is by no means an exhaustive record of Louisiana's oil history and culture, but we hope it is enough to remind the people of Louisiana of their families' important roles in building Louisiana into a vanguard of the petroleum industry.

We hope you enjoy reading this book as much as we enjoyed writing it for you.

One

Acadiana Louisiana

In early 1901, Jennings, Louisiana, was a small town of approximately 1,500 people. No paved streets existed, not even gravel roads. After the success of the Spindletop Oil Field, a group of businessmen from the Jennings area, aware of similar gas springs in the prairie northeast of Jennings, formed an oil and gas exploration company called S.A. Spencer and Company. S.A. Spencer and Company sought out the services of the Heywood brothers of Beaumont, Texas, to help drill its first well. At Scott Heywood's direction, the company chose a tract of land under its leases in the rice field of Jules Clement's farm as the location of its first well. Scott Heywood drilled that well, and on September 21, 1901, oilfield history in Louisiana began.

Jules Clement was astonished to see oil gushing from his land, and when Scott Heywood saw him standing off about 400 feet watching the gusher, he made Clement come close enough to the well "to souse him from head to foot in oil," as Heywood said. The excitement of Louisiana's first oil well brought spectators to the area, and those too close to the gusher were also showered with oil.

In his autobiography, Scott Heywood described the boom environment in Jennings as a "conglomeration of saloons, dance halls, honky-tonks, gambling houses, boarding houses, restaurants and lodging houses and all classes of people, with fights, murders and everything that usually goes on in a boom of that kind." Each driller rushed to bring in his own wells before an adjacent well could drain the oil from under his land. It was a lease-line battle with "a forest of derricks," tanks, pump stations, boiler houses, and all that went to make up a wild oil boom of the old days.

Jennings and Evangeline, Louisiana, are located in the heart of the Mamou Prairie. French immigrants settled in the area in the 1800s and brought with them the Acadian culture that is present today. These people were mostly rice farmers who also raised cattle and harvested timber from their lands. That way of life changed dramatically in 1901 with the discovery of oil atop a salt dome northeast of Jennings. (Authors' collection.)

Scott Heywood and a group of businessmen from Jennings, S.A. Spencer and Company, chose a tract of land under their oil leases in the rice field of Jules Clement's farm as the location of their first well. Clement initially agreed to drilling in his rice field but later changed his mind, worrying that his cows might fall into abandoned well holes. Heywood paid Clement $10 in advanced for any damage that might occur as a result of their drilling activities. Scott Heywood and Elmer Dobbins then began constructing the first oil well in Louisiana. (Jennings Carnegie Public Library.)

The first oil well completed in Louisiana stood out as a lone derrick in the rice fields of the Mamou Prairie, a site that would quickly change with the discovery of oil. Its completion was a source of great pride for the men who posed on the derrick floor for this picture on September 19, 1901. (Jennings Carnegie Public Library.)

On September 21, 1901, Scott Heywood brought in a gusher that spewed sand and oil for seven hours, until Jules Clement's rice field resembled a black lake. The gusher was a four-inch stream that shot up over 100 feet higher than the derrick. The oil-soused men, from left to right, are Doug Phelps, C.O. Noble, Elmer Dobbins, Saul Hendricks, and W. Scott Heywood. (Jennings Carnegie Public Library.)

The oil rush was on in Jefferson Davis and Acadia Parishes, but according to W.D. Morse, it was a "real substantial orderly boom," unlike the "wild irrational boom" following the Lucas gusher in Beaumont, Texas. Like any other boom, the culture was that of uncontrolled production. Other producers brought in wells, with almost every one of them gushing 2,500 to 10,000 barrels per day. Derricks sprang up right next to each other, pipelines crisscrossed the ground, and oil spewed over the former rice fields. (Jennings Carnegie Public Library.)

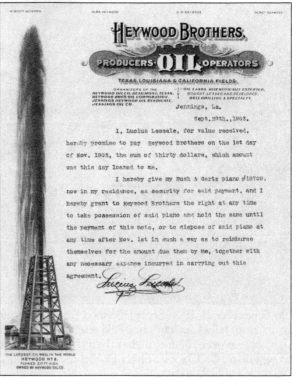

The gushing oil well was such a symbol of success and wealth that Scott Heywood's companies included it as a part of their letterhead. Heywood Oil Company boasted the largest oil well in the world, the Heywood No. 2, which flowed 217 feet high. (Jennings Carnegie Public Library.)

JENNINGS -- HEYWOOD

∾OIL SYNDICATE∾

We are doing what is done in no other field but Beaumont---
WE WILL GUARANTEE GUSHER LAND.

We Do Not Want the Earth ....

"Unless there is Oil under it."

We have the choicest Oil lands in the Jennings Oil
Field. We will make low prices and offer liberal
inducements to those desiring to assist in the development of this, the greatest oil field in the South.

OFFICERS:

Alba Heywood, President
O. W. Heywood, Vice President
I. D. L. Williams, Secretary
Frank R. Jaenke, Ass't Secretary
Avery C. Wilkins, Treasurer
T. C. Mahaffey, Ass't Treasurer

DIRECTORS:

W. Scott Heywood,
O. W. Heywood,
I. D. L. Williams,
F. R. Jaenke,
T. C. Mahaffey,
S. A. Spencer,
Alba Heywood,
Dewey Heywood

Address **Alba Heywood,** 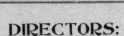 **I. D. L. Williams,**

President.　　　　　　　　　　　　　　　　　Secretary.

——JENNINGS, LOUISIANA,——

———OR———

Heywood Bros., Beaumont, Tex.

Jennings-Heywood Oil Syndicate guaranteed gusher land to its investors in a 1902 advertisement.
Interestingly, the syndicate's statement of not wanting the earth unless there is oil under it
effectively captured its lack of regard for ground surface pollution from freely discharged crude
oil. (Jennings Carnegie Public Library.)

The *Jennings Times* celebrated the city's newest industry, oil, in a special edition Sunday supplement in 1902. Rice had previously been the largest industry in Acadia, but oil quickly replaced agriculture in prosperity for the region. The images on this cover of a lounging Miss Louisiana and of the cornucopia suggest a life of ease and plenty for the people of Jennings. (Jennings Carnegie Public Library.)

Oil storage became an immediate problem in companies' desperate attempts to grab as much oil for themselves as they could before their lease neighbors got in the act. The lease-line fight that necessitated storing the massive volume of oil created an oilfield practice that became the norm throughout the field. Mexican and African American labor was imported, chiefly from Texas, to dig earthen storage tanks. At one point, 300 teams of men and mules were at work constructing earthen tanks. (Jennings Carnegie Public Library.)

The Heywood brothers started building earthen tanks and storing oil that they could not immediately sell. Other companies soon followed. This continued until over seven million barrels of oil were stored above ground in the Jennings Field. Heywood even bragged of having an earthen storage tank that held an even one million barrels of oil. (Jennings Carnegie Public Library.)

Filling the earthen tanks was a simple matter of discharging crude oil straight from the well into the open pit. Scott Heywood described oilmen in rowboats with floodlights patrolling the huge oil lakes created by the open storage reservoirs to keep ducks from landing in them. When covered in oil, the flocks of ducks would die, their carcasses clogging the intake pipes and making it impossible to transfer the oil out of the tanks to ship to market. (Jennings Carnegie Public Library.)

By 1904, the Jennings Oilfield was labeled the greatest in the history of the oil business. The Jennings Field peaked in 1906 with more than nine million barrels from its producing wells. Steel tanks were more desirable for storing and protecting oil, but their smaller sizes and higher costs compared to earthen tanks often made them less economical during the boom era of the field. (Jennings Carnegie Public Library.)

The volume of oil extracted from the Jennings Field was immense, with many wells coming in as gushers. Approximately one dozen pipes discharged oil into this small storage pit, but its capacity was quickly exceeded with the discharge of only three pipes. Crude oil splattered on the ground and in the air due to its high velocity coming out of the pipes as the men standing watch enjoyed the display of power and wealth. (Jennings Carnegie Public Library.)

Lakes of oil reflected the dozens of derricks that surrounded the open storage pits. With no lease-line laws, many neighboring derricks were owned by different oil companies. Oil storage became a community issue due to the lack of free land adjacent to each derrick. To address that problem, oil companies constructed large earthen storage tanks bordering the main field and piped the oil from their wells to those locations. They also rented space to smaller companies that did not own their own storage tanks. (Jennings Carnegie Public Library.)

The view of the Jennings Oilfield in 1907 looking north from the Texas Company oil tanks reveals a continually developing operation. The Texas Company, which later became Texaco, built several large earthen storage tanks in Section No. 47 on the Houssiere-Latrielle Oil Company land. These tanks held approximately 150,000 barrels of oil each. The local sheriff used those tanks to store sequestered oil that was held in a dispute between the Jennings-Heywood Oil Syndicate and other oil companies that went all the way to the Louisiana State Supreme Court. (Jennings Carnegie Public Library.)

A field crew digs a ditch to collect oil that has runoff from the main oil field. Ditches like this one typically had "pickup" pumps connected to hoses that returned the errant oil back to a storage tank. Scott Heywood and his company claimed all of the oil that ran into the collecting ditch they constructed in the middle of the Jennings Field, whether it came from their facilities or not. That claim ended up costing the Jennings-Heywood Oil Syndicate a large sum of money when a neighboring farmer sued the oil companies for loss of function on his land. (Jennings Carnegie Public Library.)

On July 15, 1902, the first oilfield fire in Louisiana started when lightning struck a large storage tank, igniting the Jennings Oil Company's No. 2 well. Scott Heywood and his employees constructed levees to keep the burning oil from going down the coulee that drained the oil field. Seven thousand barrels of oil per day went up in flames. It took nine days to put out the fire. (Jennings Carnegie Public Library.)

The well fire became such a spectacle that photographers and curious citizens traveled to Jennings Oilfield to view the enormous conflagration. Photographers in white shirts and hats stood only yards from the intense blaze. Ladies in white linen dresses left the site with oil stains on their parasols and clothing. (Jennings Carnegie Public Library.)

The enormous blaze melted pipes and machinery and turned the earth molten. Scott Heywood ordered steam boilers from Beaumont, Texas, to put out the fire, but they first had to arrive by train to Jennings and then by teams of 10 to 12 horses and mules to the field six miles away. While they waited for the boilers to arrive, Heywood used a fire hose to keep the fire from spreading to adjacent wells. (Jennings Carnegie Public Library.)

With four boilers from Texas and five water hoses directed at the flames, the steam plume shot 50 to 60 feet in the air. After nine days and nights of the burning inferno, Scott Heywood and his men extinguished the fire in five seconds. They used picks and shovels to dig out red molten matter from the wellhead and doused it with water to prevent the well from reigniting. The men were soaked with oil, and their eyes were so inflamed from being sprayed with oil that they were blinded for several days. (Jennings Carnegie Public Library.)

Fires were always a concern and real dangers in early oilfields with wells, derricks, and storage tanks in close proximity to each other. If a fire were not quickly brought under control, it could spread across the entire field, rapidly destroying the wooden infrastructure that held the field together. (Jennings Carnegie Public Library.)

NUMBER
5007

SHARES
100

ORGANIZED UNDER THE DECLARATION OF TRUST

Evangeline Oil Co.

FULLY PAID   CAPITAL STOCK, $6,000,000.00   NON-ASSESSABLE

This Certifies that *Thomas L. Lyman* is the owner of *One hundred* Shares of the Capital Stock of

Evangeline Oil Co.

transferable only on the books of this Corporation in person or by Attorney upon surrender of this Certificate properly endorsed.

IN WITNESS WHEREOF, the said Corporation has caused this Certificate to be signed by its duly authorized officers and its Corporate Seal to be hereunto affixed this 2nd day of Sept A.D. 1920

Vice-President   Secretary

SHARES   50 Cents   EACH

The Evangeline Oil Company, interestingly a New Jersey corporation, registered with the State of Louisiana in 1905. Its stock certificate included an etching of the Evangeline Oilfield with derricks growing in fields where rice previously grew. The illustration gives an impression of rolling hills across the Mamou Prairie; however, the grassy land was flat for as far as the eye could see. (Authors' collection.)

With Scott Heywood's discovery of oil in the Jennings Oilfield on September 21, 1901, Jennings became a boomtown. Like any other boom, the culture was that of immediate wealth, with oil companies erecting impressive buildings to house their corporate headquarters. The Houssiere-Latrielle Building housed the Houssiere-Latrielle Oil Company, pictured above, on the third floor and the Theater Ardennes on the first floor. The theater was named for the region in France from which Eugene Houssiere and Arthur Latrielle originated. The Heywood Building on Main Street, pictured below, was architecturally progressive for its time, fitting the personality of Scott Heywood. Its triangular shape, curved front, and artistic use of glass are more reminiscent of the Art Deco style of the 1920s to 1940s, yet the Heywood Brothers constructed it in the first decade of the century. (Both, authors' collection.)

In the early days of the Jennings Oilfield, operators freely discharged produced saltwater into natural waterways that farmers used for irrigation, primarily Bayou des Cannes, making the formerly fresh water useless for agricultural purposes. The Louisiana Legislature specifically created Act 183 of 1910 to address the concerns of the rice farmers of Louisiana. This law prohibited the release of "oil, saltwater, or other noxious or poisonous gas" into waterways used as sources of irrigation from March first to September first of each year, dates that corresponded with irrigation season. Above, in 1910, the water source of this rice-irrigating canal was Bayou des Cannes. Below, in 1910, water produced from the Wilkins No. 2 well flows into an open storage pit. The pit contains a weir to prevent the saltwater from entering the bayou. The presence of the weir dates the photograph between March and September of that year. (Both, authors' collection.)

Discharging saltwater from the wells directly into open fields and natural drains was the common practice in the early days of the Louisiana oil industry. According to Alba Heywood, brother of Scott Heywood, whatever negative impacts the brine had on the natural vegetation were simply a cost of doing business in the oil field. Neighboring farmers did not share that opinion. (Jennings Carnegie Public Library.)

Heifleigh completed its No. 2 well in Evangeline, Louisiana, on September 24, 1907. Lumber to build the derricks came from Mamou farmers whose lands adjoined Bayou des Cannes and who grew hearty stands of cypress trees. These farmers were able to lease their land to oil companies, sell their timber, mill it at their own sawmills, and receive oil royalties. Pictured at the Heifleigh well are, from left to right, Alie Aucoin, S.B. Ford, William Ratliff, J. Champion, O. Miller, and Z.N. Ratliff. (Jennings Carnegie Public Library.)

Crude oil gushes from a pipe into an open earthen pit at the Wilkins No. 1 well in the Jennings Field. Note the proximity of the derricks to each other. Pipelines from derricks to open settling and storage pits lie uncovered on the ground. Occupational health and safety laws did not exist in 1910; workers walking between buildings had to step over exposed pipes and puddles of oil. (Authors' collection.)

Heavy machinery with chain drives and other dangerous moving parts were essential in the early oilfields. Men wore tall leather boots and tucked in their pant legs to keep from being caught in the machines. The tall boots and long sleeves also provided protection from the intense heat and resulting burns from the steam-engine boilers. Unfortunately, these practices did not prevent men from being seriously injured or killed by the hazardous, but accepted, conditions in the "oil patch." (Jennings Carnegie Public Library.)

The Jennings Oilfield in 1906 was a dense, congested area of wooden derricks, boiler houses, cypress oil storage tanks, and simple wooden shacks. Steam rose from the boiler houses, oil puddled on

the ground, and pipes connected each segment of the field's operations. The field was hot, dirty, and noisy, and everyone wanted a piece of it. (Jennings Carnegie Public Library.)

Dobbins Iron Works and Oil City Iron Works were neighbors on East Market Street before the great fire of November 1901. Inside these modern, wood-framed buildings, men fabricated the most up-to-date equipment to meet the needs of the expanding Jennings Oilfield. Interestingly, horses and wagons still had to deliver that heavy metal equipment to the oilfields. (Jennings Carnegie Public Library.)

November 4, 1901, nearly marked the end of the Jennings business section. The fire started at 3:45 a.m. and destroyed nearly all of the commercial structures, including Dobbins Iron Works. Machine parts, casing pipe, and a workbench were all that was left of Elmer Dobbins's business. The estimated loss in property damage in 1902 was $198,275. (Jennings Carnegie Public Library.)

Elmer Dobbins, together with the Heywood brothers, opened a new iron works company in Jennings on April 14, 1902, to supply boilers, engines, and fittings to the new oil industry. The Heywoods established businesses in every aspect of the oil trade to make as much money as possible during the boom years. In addition to drilling, operating, and iron works, they had businesses for lease holdings, pipelines, storage tanks, and barges to acquire, hold, and move oil. (Jennings Carnegie Public Library.)

Oil Field Shop, Jennings Oil Field year 1906

Around 1906, Union Iron Works established a shop in the Jennings Oilfield to be closer to its customers. Shutting down a drilling operation because the necessary equipment had to be transported from Jennings was expensive. On-site ironworkers and machinists allowed the oil companies, drillers, and suppliers to be more profitable in the high-risk business of drilling for oil. (Jennings Carnegie Public Library.)

James Daniel English Sr., left, and unidentified, right, stand on the floor of the Fred I. Getty well. Getty developed and received a patent for a screen fitting for casing pipes to prevent sand from cutting off groundwater flow into irrigation wells. He later modified that fitting for use in oil wells in the Jennings Field to prevent sand from choking in the wells. (Jennings Carnegie Public Library.)

The drilling of the Southern Petroleum Company's Bryan No. 1 well was complete. Bill Webb's crew from Damon, Texas, staged dozens of casing pipe sections and joints at the front of the derrick for lining the borehole. The boiler blew steam for the engines to begin the process of extracting oil from the salt dome. A woman with a folder of papers in her hand posed with the crew. Women's roles in the oilfields were generally limited to administration or services, such as laundry. (Jennings Carnegie Public Library.)

Royal Petroleum Company's refinery, opened in 1903, was the first oil refinery in Louisiana. In 1906, Royal Petroleum put the refinery on full-scale production. Its chief commodity was alboleum, a white, tasteless, and odorless product used as an ingredient for cold cream, salves, and some medicines. It was also an excellent agent for polishing rice and for serving as a catalyst in the processing of commercial salt. Other products of the refinery included terpene, naphthalene, and phenols. (Jennings Carnegie Public Library.)

Wells in the Jennings Field were originally drilled with steam engines. Those same engines were then used to pump the oil from the ground after a well's gusher phase ended. To operate all those steam engines, a central boiler house, pictured above, was set up with pipe running to the various wells. With advancements in technology, air compressors, pictured below, replaced steam boilers. Gas engines drove the compressors, which used pressurized air to replace the steam. This enabled the old steam engines to continue to operate the wells but with a central gas engine air plant supplying the power. (Both, Jennings Carnegie Public Library.)

Immense derricks grew in fields that previously grew rice on the Mamou Prairie. The six men standing in front of this wooden derrick provide a scale to the size of the soaring structures. Oil was big business in Louisiana, requiring big construction, big machines, and big risks for the men who sought it. (Jennings Carnegie Public Library.)

Evangeline in its heyday was a popular tourist destination. Oilfields were still a novelty in Louisiana, and people would ride their carriages to the fields to view the spectacle. The woman in the lower left corner of this photograph was wearing a white dress and hat and carrying a white parasol for the occasion. Today, Evangeline resembles the prairie lands that existed before 1901, with few signs of the bustling activity and controlled chaos of its glory days. (Jennings Carnegie Public Library.)

Two

NORTHWEST LOUISIANA

Natural gas was first discovered in northwestern Louisiana in 1870 in Shreveport while drilling a water supply well for an ice plant. The gas was captured and used to light the ice plant, but it was not until the discovery of oil in Jennings in 1901 that petroleum industry excitement spread to the northwestern Louisiana parishes of Caddo, Red River, Bossier, and DeSoto. Booms in Spindletop, Texas, and Jennings, Louisiana, prompted Shreveport businessmen and Judge S.C. Fullilove, D.C. Richardson, and Ira G. Henrick to lease land in Caddo Parish to investigate gas seepages reported by area farmers.

Oil production began in northwest Louisiana in March 1905 in Caddo Field. By 1910, the Caddo Oilfield had become a significant contributor to the oil production in the state, accounting for 75 percent of its volume. Through 1942, the Caddo Field had produced approximately 1.4 billion cubic feet of natural gas and 1.6 million barrels of crude oil.

In May 1911, the Gulf Refining Company constructed the nation's first offshore oil well when it built oil-drilling rigs on barges over Caddo Lake. In addition to offshore drilling, other important petroleum firsts occurred in the oil and gas fields of northwestern Louisiana, including the first gas pipeline and the first interstate pipeline through the state.

Major oilfields in this area included Caddo, Oil City, Shreveport, Cedar Grove, and Elm Grove. Many of these fields continue to produce today.

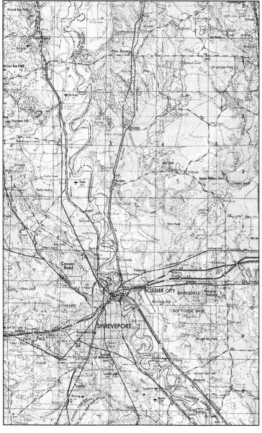

Brothers J.S. and W.A. Savage and Dr. Frank Morrical brought in the Savage No. 1 well on March 28, 1905, making it one of the first wells in the Caddo Field. They drilled the well on the Caddo Lake Oil & Pipeline Company lease in Section No. 1, Township No. 20, Range No. 16. When the well came in, it produced about five barrels of oil. They continued drilling the well deeper and deeper in an attempt to increase production but eventually abandoned it due to lack of production. Shortly after they abandoned Savage No. 1, the Texas Company drilled the first big producer in the area. (Louisiana State University, Shreveport.)

This 1955 US Geological Survey (USGS) topographic map illustrates the Caddo Pine Island Oilfield and the smaller surrounding fields. Much of the area that was not covered by cities or towns, and even part of the area that was, at one time produced oil or supported wildcat wells. The map designates many areas as "oil field" or "oil well" surrounding Shreveport and Caddo Lake. (Authors' collection.)

The Hunter Oil Well was one of many wells drilled near Shreveport, Louisiana, in the early 1900s by the Hunter Oil Company, which would later complete the first well in nearby Arkansas. The gas escaping from the well gives the appearance of boiling water. In the early days of oil exploration in northwestern Louisiana, large volumes of natural gas posed a challenge to drilling crews and often led to large blowouts of many early wells. By 1907, nearly 70 million cubic feet of natural gas were wasted daily as it blew out of the wells. In order to keep the waste down and utilize the gas, the first natural gas pipeline in Louisiana was laid from the Caddo Field to Shreveport. (Authors' collection.)

In 1910, the W.P. Stiles No. 107 well was brought in, producing around 12,000 barrels per day. The roughnecks were decked out in slickers and hats to keep the showers of oil off themselves. In many pictures from this time, the crews are wearing only their regular work clothes, so this crew was well outfitted for the job. (Louisiana State University, Shreveport.)

In 1910, the Gulf Refining Company acquired the first lease to drill for oil on Caddo Lake. The lease cost $30,000 and required intense negotiating with the levee board. Gulf drilled the oil wells from rigs on barges, and in May 1911, the first offshore well in the country, Ferry Lake No. 1, was completed. By the end of the year, Gulf had eight more wells on Caddo Lake. Some of the wells were connected by catwalks above the lake. (Louisiana State Oil and Gas Museum.)

This postcard, likely made around 1910, shows a typical scene from oil wells near Shreveport. By 1910, the oilfields of northwestern Louisiana had become major contributors to oil production, accounting for 75 percent of the state's production. The postcard shows an oil derrick surrounded by the standard production equipment, including storage tanks, pipelines, and earthen pits ringed with levees. (Authors' collection.)

Around May 1911, D.W. Harrell, a director in the Waguespack Oil and Land Developing Company, told interested parties at the St. Charles Hotel in New Orleans that the Caddo Field had in the Harrell No. 7 well on the Producer's Oil Company tract the second largest oil well in the world. Very soon after this, the well caught on fire. This was not the only well on fire in the Caddo Field at that time. For $1 per trip, the Kansas City Southern Railroad offered tours from Shreveport to view all of the well fires. (Louisiana State Oil and Gas Museum.)

The well fire at Producer's Harrell No. 7 burned from May 12 to June 6, 1911. After multiple unsuccessful attempts to extinguish the fire, digging was commenced on a 15-foot-deep, 50-foot-long tunnel heading toward the well. The intention of the tunnel was to reach the well below the surface and cut off the flow of oil. Pictured on May 21, 1911, tunnel contractor H.H. Hair and miners posed at the entrance to the tunnel. It was said that prior to the fire, this well produced as much as 75,000 barrels per day. After the fire, the production decreased to approximately 18,000 barrels per day. Unfortunately for the owners of the well, it was not producing long before it suddenly stopped spurting oil and began to gush salt water instead. (Louisiana State University, Shreveport.)

Spouting oil wells were not the only things catching on fire in the oilfields. This oil storage tank caught on fire, possibly from a lightning strike. These types of fires often had to burn themselves out because they were too difficult to extinguish. (Louisiana State Oil and Gas Museum.)

Vivian was a boomtown located in the northern portion of Caddo Field. Like many oilfields in Louisiana, the land where the wells were being drilled had been farmland or pasture. Many farmers leased their property to the oil companies and continued cultivating the land or using it as pasture, requiring the two industries to utilize the property simultaneously. (Louisiana State Oil and Gas Museum.)

Vivian was a stop along the Kansas City Southern Railroad line. This photograph, which was likely taken in the early 1900s, shows that oil workers were often proud of their oilfield finds and would pose for photographs alongside gushers or within pools of oil. (Authors' collection.)

William Thomas Bell was born in Lancaster County, South Carolina, in 1886. He began working in the oilfields as a young man in Corsicana, Texas. He met and married Annie Daniels, and they moved to Vivian, Louisiana, in 1911. Tom Bell drilled his first well in Trees City. Many men of all ages gathered to take this photograph with an oil derrick on a Tom Bell lease. (Louisiana State Louisiana, Shreveport.)

Annie (Daniels) Bell poses on the Hart's Ferry Bridge over the northern portion of Caddo Lake and Jeems Bayou. This was a favorite location for photographers to capture the charm of Jeems Bayou near its entrance into Caddo Lake. (Louisiana State Louisiana, Shreveport.)

Another well brought in by Tom Bell was this gusher near Vivian, Louisiana. It appears that this well was located in an agricultural field. Tom Bell worked in the oilfields in Louisiana and Texas for 50 years, during which he drilled over 100 wells. (Louisiana State University, Shreveport.)

Tom Bell, far right, and his drilling crew brought in the Gray 1 No. 2 well. A young girl, Nettie Lou, and her puppy, Rowdy, happily join the crew on the derrick floor of the successful well. (Louisiana State University, Shreveport.)

The Standard Oil Co's Hardie No. 2. Brought in by the B&O Driller. April 29-1911. Sims Linderman Photo.

B&O Driller brought in Standard Oil Company's Hardie No. 2 on April 29, 1911. The density of the trees around this well suggests it was not in one of the more developed areas of the Caddo–Pine Island Oil Field. The photographer was brought in specifically to capture the spectacular gushing of the oil over the top of the derrick. (Louisiana State Oil and Gas Museum.)

Oil City was the center of activity in the Caddo Oil Field. According to this 1912 photograph, Oil City had many businesses that supported the oil industry, including an attorney at law, who would have been instrumental in property leases. To support and entertain the oilfield workers, Oil City offered a smokehouse and billiards hall. (Louisiana State Oil and Gas Museum.)

Oilfield fires posed large problems in the early years of production in northwestern Louisiana, not only due to the large amount of natural gas in the wells but also because of the lack of ability to fight these large fires. The 1913 fire at the Star Oil Co. Loucke No. 3 well in Caddo Oilfield was the largest single well fire in the country at that time. Crews eventually extinguished the fire by driving a truck into the flames to bend a pipe, redirecting the oil into an earthen storage pit. (Library of Congress.)

This photograph in the Caddo Oilfield in 1913 is titled "C.O. Company Lindsey No. 1 well, Bob Ferguson & Crew." The C.O. Company was likely the Caddo Oil Company. Whereas most of the photographs of crews on derricks show the well and the derrick in the frame to emphasize the stream of oil gushing from the top, this photograph has an up-close view of the drilling platform. (Louisiana State Oil and Gas Museum.)

Mooringsport, like Oil City and Vivian, was a boomtown, though the town did exist prior to the oil boom. Mooringsport was located on the south side of the east arm of Caddo Lake, and the lake can be seen in the background of this photograph. This scene of Mooringsport from May 1913 shows the houses in the town built amongst the derricks. (Louisiana State Oil and Gas Museum.)

In 1913, driller Tom Barnett, fourth from right on the bottom row, and his crew are "rigging up" on Gulfy's Hunsicker No. 4. The Gulf Oil Company was at one time the Guffy Oil Company, which is likely where the nickname "Gulfy" comes from. "Hunsicker" was likely the owner of the property where the well was drilled. (Louisiana State Oil and Gas Museum.)

A tubing gang of the Gulf Oil Company near Vivian, Louisiana, sits on top of a wooden storage tank in the Caddo–Pine Island Field around 1913. It appears that the tanks throughout the photograph are submerged in water, suggesting that the area was flooded at the time. A pipeline crosses behind the men, most likely to the derrick in the background. (Louisiana State Oil and Gas Museum.)

The first interstate gas pipeline was laid from the Caddo Oilfield to Marshall, Texas, in 1906, and the first interstate oil pipeline was constructed from Oklahoma through the Caddo Field to Baton Rouge in 1910. From that point forward, many pipelines were laid throughout the state and between other states. This pipeline crew is taking a dinner break in the Caddo Oilfield in 1915. Notice the dog in the background sitting up with what looks like a hat on. (Louisiana State Oil and Gas Museum.)

In 1915, the Gulf Refining Company brought in a gusher that produced approximately 25,000 barrels per day on the Boyter lease near Vivian, Louisiana. The Gulf Refining Company had underestimated the potential of this well and only constructed tanks for 250 barrels. The tanks would have been similar to these cypress receiving tanks. Prior to this well coming in, the largest producer in the Caddo Oilfield had been 20,000 barrels per day. (Louisiana State Oil and Gas Museum.)

The fishtail drilling bit was the first bit type developed for rotary drilling, which has been the primary method of drilling in Louisiana. These men in the Caddo Oilfield are dressing the bit, forming it to the proper shape. This type of drill bit worked by rotating and grinding away the ground as water or drilling mud passed to the bit. (Louisiana State Oil and Gas Museum.)

In 1919, a newspaper advertisement aimed at attracting investors in a northwestern Louisiana oil company quoted Commissioner M.L. Alexander of the Louisiana Department of Conservation, stating "the recent discoveries in the northern sections of the state lead to the belief that the whole commonwealth is under laid with a vast sea of oil and a gas chamber of unknown capacity." The drilling crews on these wells from that time period were part of the rush to tap into the sea of oil. (Above: Louisiana State University, Shreveport; below: Louisiana State Oil and Gas Museum.)

The Bossier Oilfield was founded in 1908. As the picture states, the field had a shallow pool, which meant wells did not have to be drilled as deeply as in some other fields. The National Oil Company and Standard Oil Company were two of the major producers in the field. (Louisiana State University, Shreveport.)

Jeems (or James) Bayou was the waterway that fed Caddo Lake. This over-water well near Stacey's Landing south of Trees, Louisiana, had a boardwalk connecting it either to the shore or to another well. Additional over-water derricks can be seen in the background. (Louisiana State University, Shreveport.)

World War I greatly increased the demand for oil, leading to wildcatting in search of new fields. The search led to the discovery of the Pine Island Field, which brought about a new boom for northwest Louisiana in 1916. The Pine Island Deep Sand Well was drilled on the R.K. Smith Lease in the 1920s. H.D. Easton was the geologist. (Louisiana State University, Shreveport.)

With the high rate of oil and gas extraction in northwest Louisiana, pipelines were necessary to carry the raw product to refineries for processing. In the Caddo Oilfield in 1917, E.E. Swanson and the Gulf Pipeline work crew took a break from laying pipelines to pose for this photograph at their camp. The gentleman in the front row is holding a rope from one of the tents in the camp. (Louisiana State Oil and Gas Museum.)

With the number of wells producing oil in the Caddo Field in the early 1920s, something had to be done about oil storage. Those who profited according to the volume of oil produced wanted to get the oil out of the ground before somebody on a neighboring property drained it out from under them. But, in order to keep the price of oil from plummeting, they could not put all of the oil on the market. The storage solution was to direct oil to tanks made of steel, wood, or earth, like the one shown here. (Louisiana State Oil and Gas Museum.)

Crude oil extracted from the field required processing for its use in various products. Oil from the well sites or from storage tanks was taken to treatment plants. The Gulfey Treatment Plant near Vivian, Louisiana, likely processed oil from the nearby Caddo Oilfield. Gulfey was likely the Gulf Refining Company, which was prominent in the area. The young children appear comfortable amongst the workers and the oilfield equipment at the plant. (Louisiana State Oil and Gas Museum.)

In the early 1920s, the Bull Bayou Oilfield was considered second in importance to the Homer Oilfield. Bull Bayou Field was located south of Shreveport near the Red River. On the left, the Red River is seen in the background and the train station and town are in the foreground. Oil derricks and tents from oilfield camps are scattered throughout, and a burning well can even be seen toward the right. Additionally, this view of the Bull Bayou Oilfield shows how oil and

The Homer Oilfield was located in Claiborne Parish, approximately 50 miles northeast of Shreveport. The Consolidated Progressive Oil Company of New York completed the first well in the Homer Field, Shaw No. 1, in January 1919. Homer Field turned out major gushers in the early 1920s, giving it the nickname "Wonder Pool." Oil was extracted so quickly that construction of pipelines could not keep up with the flow. Producers hurriedly erected tank farms to handle all of the production. This bird's-eye view of the Homer Oilfield shows the expansiveness of the field. Oil derricks can be seen far into the distance. The derricks are labeled with names of

farming industries coexisted. Agricultural fields stretch throughout this photograph, with oil derricks, tanks, camps, and equipment scattered amongst them. A fortunate property owner could profit from both the minerals below the surface and the fertile soil on the surface. These panoramic views of oilfields give a sense of the density of the derricks and the layout of an oilfield in northwestern Louisiana in the early 1920s. (Library of Congress.)

some of the major producers in the field, including the Gulf Refining Company, Gilliland and Foster, Standard Oil Company, and Simms Oil Company. The photograph is also evidence of how productive the field was in the early 1920s, with production rates labeled for some wells in the range of 10,000 to 34,000 barrels per day. In the background of the photograph, the camps, which were developed to house workers of the oil companies, are also labeled. The Standard Oil Company is shown toward the left, and Simms Oil Company camps are in the center to the right. (Library of Congress.)

North of the Homer Oilfield, almost to the Arkansas border, was the Haynesville Oilfield. A large crowd was present for the bringing in of the Anna Taylor well in 1921. It was said that the total royalty income of the Anna Taylor was in the neighborhood of $1,000 a day during this time. In Haynesville in the early 1920s, there were many rags-to-riches stories of poor landowners who became wealthy with royalty payments. (Louisiana State Oil and Gas Museum.)

A similarly large crowd gathers around this well in the Caddo Oilfield in 1920. Many bystanders drove to the field to get a close view of the working rig. The liquid spraying out on the left is not deterring the viewers from getting close to the well. (Louisiana State Oil and Gas Museum.)

This is a view of Caddo Lake on June 12, 1923. In the foreground, what appears to be a metal derrick on a wooden platform towers over a well being pumped near the shore. Additional wells can be seen in the background, both on land and offshore. The Gulf Oil Company drilled over 250 wells in the bed of Caddo Lake. (Louisiana State Oil and Gas Museum.)

A flowing oil well in the Caddo–Pine Island Field in the early 1920s drenched the men who were connecting it in oil. The men are working hard to stop the oil from flowing over the derrick floor, which appears slick with oil. (Louisiana State Oil and Gas Museum.)

Oil City was bordered on the southwest by Caddo Lake and on the northeast by Clear Lake. In 1956, Clear Lake overtopped its banks and flooded the city. Floodwaters submerge all of the derricks in the oilfields in the top right; the town and oilfields in the bottom left are dry. Even today, when driving though Oil City, oil pumps can be seen in the yards of homes and throughout the town. (Louisiana State Oil and Gas Museum.)

Three

COASTAL AND OFFSHORE LOUISIANA

The development of the offshore oil industry in Louisiana began inland in the Lake Caddo Field of northwestern Louisiana in the 1910s. Offshore literally meant no attachment to the shore, as was the situation for drilling rigs and derricks built on piles in the lake bottoms. The offshore term shifted to coastal Louisiana in the 1930s and 1940s with well sites drilled in the marshes and bayous and in the Gulf of Mexico in water depths up to 20 feet.

Offshore oil exploration in Louisiana took off after World War II. Many of the early companies, formed by local entrepreneurs familiar with the marshes and near-shore Gulf, supplied specialty services to support the nascent offshore industry. Large oil and gas companies from other states sought their local expertise in traversing the marshes and near-shore waters to develop new oilfields.

Hurricanes in the Gulf of Mexico were larger threats than ever before as the industry turned to aquatic fields in search of new deposits. Kerr-McGee and Phillips Petroleum completed the first out-of-sight-of-land well in 1947 off the coast of Morgan City, marking a new phase in the offshore industry. Alden J. "Doc" Laborde soon followed with his patented design for a movable offshore oil rig capable of drilling in 40-foot water depths. Today, oil patch families carry on the pride of their ancestors as Louisiana adds to its offshore oil legacy with rigs capable of drilling off the continental shelf.

This c. 1937 promotional book for southern Louisiana illustrates the riches that could be had for those investing in or moving to the Gulf Coast. The derrick gushes oil over a quaint house as people gather on the derrick floor. The palm tree adds a tropical touch to a paradise that coexisted with oil operations. (Tulane University.)

The first submerged oil wells were drilled from platforms built on piers in Caddo and Pine Island in the 1910s. Gulf Oil drilled the world's first oil well in inland waters at Caddo Lake in 1911. This was the first truly "offshore" well, detached completely from the shore. Subsequently, drilling occurred in the lakes, marshes, and bayous of other parts of Louisiana beginning in the 1920s. (Louisiana State Oil and Gas Museum; donated by First National Bank.)

In the area of Sulphur, Louisiana, in Calcasieu Parish, oil was not the first exploited mineral. Sulfur, as the name of the town suggests, was first mined in the 1870s and last mined in the area in 1924. Later in the 1920s, the Union Sulfur Company converted from sulfur to oil production. This 1925 photograph shows a group of oil derricks in the Sulphur area. (State Library of Louisiana.)

The Bayou Sale Field in St. Mary Parish in coastal Louisiana was discovered on the eve of Pearl Harbor in 1941. This is the Humble Oil company town in Bayou Sale near Morgan City in 1944. In the foreground is the recreation hall with a screened barbeque pit behind it. The camp homes lie beyond it. (State Library of Louisiana.)

Development of the Vinton-Ged Oilfield began in 1910, when Leonard Beckenstein traveled to Ged to obtain an oil lease. He met with John Geddings Gray, the farmer and landowner of an area reportedly with so much oil that it was present in the horse watering troughs. The men discussed the oil deal over a bottle of Cascade Whiskey, naming the new venture the Cascade Lease. (McNeese State University.)

A new icon of oilfield success appeared and was soon known by many names: nodding donkey, horsehead pump, rocking horse, beam pump, sucker rod pump, grasshopper pump, thirsty bird, and popping johnny. The oil pump jack, as it was formally called, pulled oil from the Vinton-Ged Field by mechanically lifting liquid out of the well when sufficient bottom hole pressure did not exist to flow liquid all the way to the surface. (McNeese State University.)

Cypress trees and knees and oil derricks coexisted in 1944 in the swamps of south Louisiana. Drillers typically cleared an area for access and well pads, leaving the surrounding vegetation undisturbed. Oil has historically been prevalent in coastal Louisiana because of the wetland environment with its high organic soil content. (Authors' collection.)

The Pure Oil Company established an oil camp in Gueydan that contained six houses, storage and office buildings, a car garage, and a mechanic shop. A rope swing hung inside the water tower. The drilling lease was approximately one mile from the camp. Eight to ten wells were on that lease, including the Alliance No. 2. Gueydan was a relatively poor community, with oil people held in high esteem, as they made more money than farmhands. During World War II, residents of Gueydan held scrap metal drives, obtaining metal from the drilling rigs to help the war effort. (McNeese State University.)

THROUGH THIS DOOR

the oilman passes—
assured of a warm
welcome and consideration
of his financial problems.

Offices at

LAKE CHARLES, LA.

WELSH, LA.	JENNINGS, LA.
OAKDALE, LA.	VINTON, LA.
SULPHUR, LA.	DeQUINCY, LA.
KINDER, LA.	LAKE ARTHUR, LA.
ELTON, LA.	OBERLIN, LA.

THE
CALCASIEU-MARINE NATIONAL BANK

LAKE CHARLES, LOUISIANA

The Calcasieu-Marine National Bank catered to the oilman and his business, as seen in this 1950s newspaper advertisement. Its main office was located on Ryan Street in Lake Charles in a grand building that is now in the National Register of Historic Places. Its 11 offices were located mainly in coastal cities with well-established oilfields and associated supply businesses. (Jennings Carnegie Public Library.)

The Cit-Con oil refinery was the first of its kind in the United States when it opened in 1949, employing approximately 750 people. With a construction cost of $42 million, it was the largest high-temperature oil refinery in the world, extracting 6,000 barrels of lubricating oil a day from 18,000 barrels of crude. (Authors' collection.)

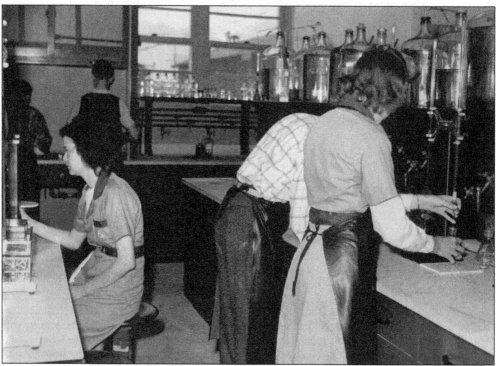

The petroleum industry developed as a man's line of work, but the Cities Service butadiene plant in Lake Charles employed several women in its laboratory as part of the war effort. The *Lake Charles American Press* featured a "Cities Service Refinery Section" in the May 26, 1944, issue to mark the official beginning of operations of "the world's newest and most modern oil refinery." According to the article, the refinery would operate at a rate that would "supply daily aviation gasoline for 1,000 bombers on the London to Berlin run." (McNeese State University.)

Engineers with Higgins, Inc., created prototype models of offshore oil rigs for laboratory testing before turning over their designs to welders and other construction professionals. Nozzles and hoses allowed engineers to create pressure and wave environments typical in offshore waters to determine the stability of their designs. Tests performed on this model were for towing the platform to the offshore drill site, as indicated by the derrick lying on its side. (University of New Orleans.)

A barge transports the completed offshore platform base from Higgins's construction facilities on the Industrial Canal in New Orleans with the help of two tugboats. This base, which was approximately 50 feet tall, 35 feet wide, and 35 feet long, was the culmination of thousands of hours of labor. Workers stood on the dock watching its departure with pride. (University of New Orleans.)

Building the massive steel structures required extensive coordination with engineers, welders, and crane operators. Because of its height, workers built the top portion of a platform lying on its side. The darker-colored steel was an extension of the base shown in the previous image and remained underwater. The lighter colored steel was the portion of the rig that remained above the water level. Crew and supply boats tied up next to the ladder and climbed to the grated rig deck. (University of New Orleans.)

It was time for a coffee break on a Humble Oil rig in Bayou Sale, St. Mary Parish, in 1944. The men used steam from the rig to brew their coffee, making good use of limited resources while in a remote location in coastal Louisiana. (State Library of Louisiana.)

Inside the rig, the galley was as busy as the drill floor. Good food was essential for the morale of the crew stationed offshore for weeks at a time. Supply boats had to bring in all utensils, cookware, and ingredients. Fishing off the platform also provided fresh seafood for the cooks to prepare, and food scraps thrown overboard provided incentives for sea creatures to continue foraging around the rig. (International Petroleum Museum & Exposition.)

High atop a rig over the marshes of south Louisiana, welder Chuck Gill takes time out for a coffee break. With one hand on the rigging and one hand on the coffee cup, Gill illustrates the dexterity, balance, and nerve required of early offshore workers. Casing pipe and tool joints wait on the barge for him to finish his break. (McNeese State University.)

Offshore living was communal living, with all facilities in close quarters. Older rigs like *Mr. Charlie* provided living space for 58 crewmembers. Each small bedroom contained two bunk beds stacked three beds high and one desk and chair. A separate locker room, pictured above, provided closet space for personal items. One community bathroom with three sinks and three stalls, pictured below, was available for the crew of 58 men. Crewmembers worked around the clock in three shifts to keep the drilling operations running, thereby rotating the need for shower and bathroom facilities. (Both, International Petroleum Museum & Exposition.)

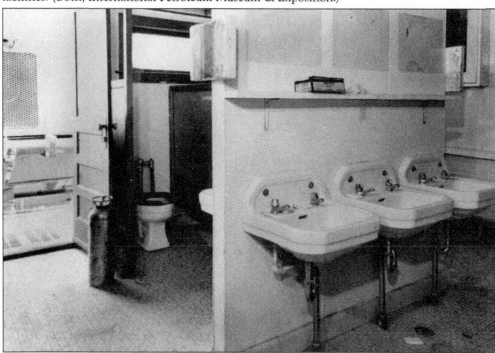

Mechanical jobs on oil rigs included working in the tight spaces of the engine room. Engine rooms were hot, noisy, cramped, and hazardous, and they contained all the heavy equipment not required to be on the drilling deck. Note the oil splattering from the valves and tubes above as the machine runs to produce the energy required for drilling, electricity, and cooling aboard the rig. The engine room inside the barge, pictured below, contains the electric generators, mud pumps, cement pumps, fuel tanks, fuel pumps, ballast tanks, ballast pumps, and cement tanks. (Both, International Petroleum Museum & Exposition.)

Under the drill floor lies the "moon pool." Moon pools originated in the oil drilling industry because of the need to pass drilling equipment into the water from a platform or drillship. Drill pipes need to run vertically through the structure or hull, and the moon pool provides the means to do this. The moon pool on *Mr. Charlie* shows that the blowout preventer and other safety equipment are in place. (International Petroleum Museum & Exposition.)

The mud sack room of an offshore drilling rig contains 100-pound bags of barite drilling mud stacked to the ceiling. One of the most critical roles of drilling mud is as a lubricant. Drilling generates tremendous friction, which can damage the drill or the formation being drilled. Drilling mud cuts down on the friction, lowering the heat of drilling and reducing the risk of friction-related complications. The mud also acts as a carrier for the materials being drilled, which become suspended in the mud and are carried up the drill to the surface. (International Petroleum Museum & Exposition.)

Shell Oil Company wanted to open a field at the mouth of the Mississippi River, but it determined that such a field would not be cost-effective with its traditional build-and-drill methods. Alexander Shipyard in New Orleans had recently completed *Mr. Charlie* in late 1953, and Shell hired the rig to open the field. *Mr. Charlie* floated from New Orleans to the Gulf of Mexico deployment at East Bay Field in 1954 with the help of one tugboat. (International Petroleum Museum & Exposition.)

Mr. Charlie was the first transportable, submersible drilling rig capable of drilling wells in water depths up to 40 feet. The brainchild of Alden J. "Doc" Laborde, *Mr. Charlie*'s barge was approximately 220 feet long and 85 feet wide. Under the living quarters, pontoons extended the width to 136 feet. *Mr. Charlie* was named after Charles H. Murphy, a cotton ginner, banker, and oil man whose determination and perseverance so inspired his son, the owner of Murphy Oil Corporation, that after providing the initial $500,000 investment in the rig, he named it for his father. (International Petroleum Museum & Exposition.)

"Doc" Laborde, a young US Navy engineer working at Kerr-McGee, had an idea that a self-sufficient drilling rig could be installed on a transportable barge and floated to any location in water depths up to 40 feet. In late 1953, his idea became a reality as *Mr. Charlie*. The staff gage on the submersible portion of the rig tracked the water depth as the barge descended under the water. The deepest hole dug by *Mr. Charlie* was 22,840 feet. (International Petroleum Museum & Exposition.)

The Union Producing Company No. 1 well, 18 miles south of Morgan City, was drilling at a gas horizon of approximately 12,500 feet with 6,500 pounds of pressure on the "Christmas Tree," the assembly of valves, spools, and fittings used to control the flow of gas. A mistake was made while running the storm choke in the tubing string, resulting in a fire that destroyed the barge. Storm chokes were used in offshore applications as contingency devices in the event of a catastrophic failure of surface facilities during a storm or hurricane. (McNeese State University.)

A "monster at rest," McDermott's derrick barge No. 7 returns to Morgan City for supplies and repairs. The barge was 300 feet long and 90 feet wide, and its crane lifted 250 tons. First introduced by J. Ray McDermott in 1949, this type of vessel changed the direction of the offshore construction industry. Instead of constructing oil platforms in parts, jackets and decks could be built onshore as modules. (McNeese State University.)

Kerr-McGee mobile rig No. 47 drills for Phillips Petroleum in the Eugene Isle area, 40 miles south of Morgan City. Ingalls SB built the submersible rig in 1957 in Pascagoula, Mississippi. The number of offshore mobile units increased from one in 1949, drilling in 20 feet of water, to an estimated 150 by the end of 1966, drilling in 1,000 feet of water. (McNeese State University.)

Through the years, Mobil was among the largest sellers of gasoline and motor oils in the United States and held the top spot during the 1940s and much of the 1950s. One of Mobil Oil Company's oil production platforms was located in the Eugene Isle area, 40 miles south of Morgan City. By 2006, the Gulf of Mexico hosted 3,858 oil and gas platforms. (McNeese State University.)

When the total borehole depth has been reached, all of the drill string must be pulled out of the hole to run in casing pipe. Roughnecks standing on the rotary table, above, wait for the tool joint to come through. Once it appears, they break (unscrew) the tool joint, below, between the two pairs of tongs. (Both, McNeese State University.)

The stand of pipe, a forble (four lengths of drill pipe connected to form a section, which is handled and stacked in a derrick as a single unit on borehole round trips), has been broken (unscrewed), and the pipe racker, "Fox" Sexton, racks it back in its slot. (McNeese State University.)

The rig floor appears to be a cluttered area of pipe work, hoses, holes, and tools, but it serves as a safe area where operators can handle or joint the drill string parts. From left to right, Chuck Gill, "Hooks" Chapman, and Lawrence Pedigo take a break from their drilling work. The hot and dirty conditions in which they work are evident on their sweat-stained clothes. (McNeese State University.)

Surveying the marshes of Louisiana for pipeline routes required swamp buggies to tow platforms through the unstable coastal land to obtain bearings and distances. The large, open wheels pushed down the vegetation and attempted to minimize getting stuck in the soft mud. When buggies did get stuck, men had to walk on the back wheels to get them moving again. Marsh buggies were also used to lay pipelines across the marsh. Pipes were first coated so they would float, then loaded on large Styrofoam floats with draglines. Marsh buggies pulled the floats as workers welded and pushed the line out. When the pipeline was complete, they cut off the floats, and the pipe settled into the ditch dug by the dragline. (Both, McNeese State University.)

Hurricane Audrey struck Cameron Parish in June 1957. Damage in Louisiana was catastrophic, with 60 to 80 percent of the homes and businesses from Cameron to Grand Chenier destroyed or severely damaged. The damage from all offshore oil facilities totaled $16 million (1957 dollars). Storm surge inundated oilfields in Cameron, flattening derricks and overflowing production pits. (Both, McNeese State University.)

Four

OIL TRANSPORTATION

The Louisiana petroleum industry utilized nearly every mode of transportation available to explore, access, and distribute its oil. In the early days, horses, mules, and oxen pulled wagons laden with casing pipe, boilers, and steam engines through muddy unpaved roads and sticky swamps. As oilfields and boomtowns grew, rail lines and pipelines connected them to markets across the state and throughout the country. The abundance of Louisiana oil contributed to a wider interest in and accessibility to the combustion-engine automobile. Motorized trucks delivered heating oil to residential neighborhoods, and the ever-helpful service station attendant became a ubiquitous fixture of highway travel.

Oil exploration advanced into previously difficult-to-access regions with the invention of the marsh buggy and the floatplane. Submersible barges carried transportable drilling rigs offshore into increasing water depths. Natural gas pipelines allowed that previously wasted resource to become a viable energy alternative across state lines. Louisiana refined its extracted petroleum products for both world wars for use in tanks and bombers.

Advances in the transportation industry contributed to advances in the petroleum industry and vice versa. This symbiotic relationship continues today with the development of more efficient fuel blends and vehicles powered by hybrid engines.

Louisiana was a state with countless bayous, streams, and rivers, making ferries important modes of transportation for delivering machinery to early Louisiana oilfields. This Red River ferry was just long enough to accommodate the two-teamed, six-wheeled wagon required to bring a boiler to the remote oil field. Mud on the wagon wheels attests to the poor road conditions through which men and animals had to travel to supply the fields. (Louisiana State University, Shreveport.)

In 1923, going "off-tour" had the same meaning as "off-road" does today. Three unfortunate men at Oilton went "off-tour" with their light wagon and were stuck in the mud long enough to have their picture taken. The oil field, safe from the floodwaters, remained active with smoke from its boilers billowing around wooden derricks and storage tanks. (Louisiana State Oil and Gas Museum; donated by Shelby Ogletree.)

A log wagon purchased from the Fruge Brothers' sawmill near Hathaway, Louisiana, gained new life hauling boilers from Jennings to Evangeline. The old-style boiler on this wagon was first used in 1901 in the Evangeline Oilfield for drilling shallow oil wells. By 1908, larger boilers, called 45s, replaced the smaller, original boilers. (Jennings Carnegie Public Library.)

A five-teamed wagon prepares to haul oilfield machinery from the railroad depot in the town of Jennings to the Jennings Oilfield, roughly six miles away. Jennings had many modern amenities, including railroads, electricity, and fire hydrants, as a result of the oil boom, but its roads were still unpaved. Wagon tracks crisscross the muddy depot at South Broadway and East Railroad Avenues. (Jennings Carnegie Public Library.)

Multi-teamed wagons carrying boiler parts and casing pipes were spectacles on neighborhood streets. Pedestrians stopped along the sidewalk as an eight-teamed wagon passed by affluent homes en route to the oil field. The number of mules needed to pull the wagon indicates the weight of the boiler. (Louisiana State Oil and Gas Museum.)

86

By the 1920s, wheels on oilfield wagons were wider to better traverse the difficult roads and sloppy field conditions. Despite this improvement, wagons still sank in the oilfield mud. Perhaps the two men riding the steam boiler were just enough extra weight to bog down the wagon. The men guiding (and riding) the wagon team are, from left to right, Durham Matthews, unidentified, Robert Player, and unidentified. (Louisiana State Oil and Gas Museum.)

Transporting machinery became easier after railroads connected towns to remote oilfields. In the Caddo Oilfield around 1910, men lined up their wagons next to a flatbed railcar to offload oil well gears and steam boilers. Transferring equipment from the rail lines to individual well sites still required horses and wagons. The elevated pipeline filled tanker cars with crude oil for distribution to markets with ever-increasing numbers of "horseless carriages." (Louisiana State Oil and Gas Museum.)

Oxen similar to these were used to haul oil equipment before motorized transportation options became available. The oxen were organized in teams two oxen wide, connected by the yoke, and as many oxen long as were required to haul the weight of the load. (Jennings Carnegie Public Library.)

Even goats were used in oilfield transportation, this time to transport children of oilfield workers as they played next to an active derrick. Based on the small berm on which the goats are standing and on the sheen on the surface of the liquid, the stream the wagon is attempting to cross is most likely crude oil. The tented structure on the right is probably the home of several of these children. (Louisiana State Oil and Gas Museum.)

A Texas Company Ace truck makes deliveries of kerosene in New Orleans. Crude oil and other petroleum products were often sprayed on unpaved streets to manage dust and vegetation growth. The Texas Company, now Texaco, was one of the first oil companies from Texas to find success in Louisiana oilfields. (Library of Congress.)

With the expansion of combustion-engine automobiles into rural areas, gas stations like this Texaco station in Jennings began appearing throughout the state. Unlike today's underground storage tanks, early gas stations stored their products in large aboveground tanks. Understanding the need to brand its petroleum products, Texaco included spotlights on the ends of its storage tanks to highlight its trademark "Lone Star." (Jennings Carnegie Public Library.)

Motorized trucks replaced mule teams for transporting men and equipment to and from the oilfields. Rubber tires with (relatively) substantial treads marked a further improvement for traversing the muddy, off-road conditions. This early GMC flatbed truck hauled casing pipes and oil drenched men through north Louisiana fields. The license plate on the truck is dated 1922. (Louisiana State Oil and Gas Museum.)

G.I. Golden, providing pipe and supplies in the Jennings and Evangeline Fields, proudly carries a predecessor on its bed for the 50th anniversary of Louisiana's oil discovery in Jennings. As soon as the oil business started in Louisiana, there was a need for the trucking and supply business. Trucks moved drilling rigs for drilling onshore, all kinds of piping, and steam boilers, like the Emerson-Brantingham boiler in the parade, that were used to power the rigs. (Jennings Carnegie Public Library.)

The Caddo Lake Oilfield required barges as well as trucks to move equipment to its well sites. Water-borne transportation was less expensive than road hauling, and in many instances, it was the only option for shipping equipment to marshy oilfields. Around 1918, Federal Motor Trucks fit the needs of many operators in the oil industry with its solidly built, no-nonsense commercial models. Barge operators lined these trucks bumper to bumper for transport on the Red River. (Louisiana State Oil and Gas Museum.)

In Caddo Lake, hundreds of wells were constructed within the waters of the lake. Operators constructed catwalks to access the rigs close to shore, but to get oilfield workers to the rigs further out in the lake, crew boats were necessary. This crew boat from 1917 is loaded and ready to head out to the rigs. (Louisiana State Oil and Gas Museum.)

When the government declared Standard Oil a monopoly in 1911 and broke it into "Baby Standards," most of Louisiana was a part of Standard Oil of Ohio, which became Sohio in 1928. Standard Oil Company of Louisiana (Stancola) served eastern Louisiana around New Orleans. Standard Oil delivered the small tanks of petroleum products on this truck to local customers. Larger tank trucks and tank railcars serviced regional and interstate customers. The man on the right is A.D. Gibson, an agent for Standard Oil Company. (Louisiana State Oil and Gas Museum.)

Vivian Oil & Gasoline Company registered as a business in Louisiana in 1924 and continues today as a convenience store business. In Rodessa, Louisiana, around 1936, its Sinclair service station attendants stood ready to fill the gas tank, change the oil, and wash the windshield. Attendants staged Quaker State oilcans and filters on the service island for easy access and speedy customer service. (Louisiana State Oil and Gas Museum.)

With colorful and informative road maps, oil companies wished families "Happy Motoring!" on smooth-riding, modern asphalt highways from Maine to Louisiana. A 1950s newspaper article reported that these "free" maps cost oil and gas companies $14 million per year to produce. (Authors' collection.)

Boat passengers Bob Waddell, Mrs. J.L. Hamilton, Florence Hamilton, and a pet dog fish near Stacy Landing in the reflections of oil derricks around 1915. Boat rides to and from well sites in Caddo Lake provided dinner opportunities and leisure times for oilfield workers and their families. (Louisiana State Oil and Gas Museum.)

The east side of Mooringsport, Louisiana, a village in Caddo Parish, was an example of towns developing and expanding in the middle of active oilfields. Steel derricks that grew in place of trees surrounded wood-framed homes, and railcars brought supplies literally to the field's doorstep. While this arrangement was very economical for transporting equipment and products in and out of the oil field, it must have been difficult for families to live in such industrial environments. (Louisiana State University, Shreveport.)

Vivian, Louisiana, named for a locomotive engineer's daughter, began as a railroad stop in the early days of the north Louisiana oil boom. The steel railroad bridge that crossed Black Bayou along Gilliam-Vivian Road stood with an unusual blanket of snow in 1921. The derrick and storage tanks in the background supplied crude oil that was transported on the Kansas City Southern Railroad line that utilized this bridge. (Louisiana State Oil and Gas Museum.)

Jaenke Bridge near Jennings, Louisiana, crossed Bayou Nezpique on the main road to the oilfields from the town. All equipment shipped in on trains had to pass over this wood-pile bridge for delivery at well sites. Frank R. Jaenke was one of the original businessmen in S.A. Spencer and Company, which bought oil leases from rice farmers on the Mamou Prairie. (Authors' collection.)

96

In 1914, Midland Bridge Company constructed the Caddo Lake drawbridge, which crosses Caddo Lake at Mooringsport, to replace the ferry. The vertical-lift design of the bridge allowed tall oil equipment to pass, including the equipment used to construct the rigs in Caddo Lake. The US Army even used the bridge for training exercises to prepare soldiers for World War II. They learned to capture the bridge and bombed it with sacks of flour. (Louisiana State Oil and Gas Museum.)

Formerly used to move cement, this container car was the first of 100 to go into service as a petroleum carrier. All of the 100 cars moved kerosene from Destrehan, Louisiana, to Chelsea, Massachusetts, as part of the World War II war effort. (Library of Congress.)

By World War II, oil was so important to the US economy and to national security that young men who worked on seismic crews and drilling crews in southern Louisiana were kept home to continue their work. Much of the oil consumed in the war effort was discovered, drilled, and refined in Louisiana. Gasoline-supply soldiers fill five-gallon cans, above, directly from tank cars as part of Lt. Gen. Walter Krueger's Third Army maneuvers in Louisiana in 1941. One of the participating divisions draws its supply of gasoline from the provisional gas depot below. (Both, Library of Congress.)

Higgins, Inc., of New Orleans, famously known for its landing craft vehicle personnel (LCVPs) used in amphibious landings in the Normandy Invasion, produced marine craft and offshore oil structures after World War II. Around 1950, as part of its industrial services, Higgins, Inc., delivered Baroid drilling mud to loading docks for transfer to service boats that supplied offshore rigs. (University of New Orleans.)

Another important mode of transporting oil and gas was by pipeline. Prior to the laying of pipelines to a field, natural gas could not be captured, because there was no way to handle it. Large amounts of natural gas were lost to the atmosphere or burned off before pipelines were available to capture and transport it. From left to right, Henry Vaughn, D.W. Hadwin, E.E. Swanson, W.D. Dawson, and A.D. Whitson from the Gulf Pipeline Company laid this pipeline in the Caddo Oilfield, which was the location of the first interstate natural gas pipeline in the country. (Louisiana State Oil and Gas Museum.)

E.E. Swanson and the Gulf Pipeline crew constructed this eight-inch pipeline in the Caddo Oilfield in 1917. On the left side of the photograph, men work with a large set of tongs, which were used to assist screwing the joints together. On the right side of the photograph, a crewmember uses a pipeline jack and jack board to hold the pipes steady at the desired work level. (Louisiana State Oil and Gas Museum.)

It was not economical to zigzag pipelines to avoid muck in the swamps of northwest Louisiana, creating dirty work for a pipe layer. One of the workers in the foreground is using a pipeline jack, while another is holding the jack board, elevating the pipe above the swamp. (Louisiana State Oil and Gas Museum.)

Lake Arthur was the home of the Superior Oil Company dock for its derrick barges, including the *Supco VII*, completed on August 27, 1946. Levingston Shipbuilding from Orange, Texas, built the 92-foot tugboat. Levingston was the US Navy's leading builder of ocean tugs in World War II and continued in that market after the war. When the offshore market developed, Levingston was in the forefront, developing and building many of the early designs. It was the only US builder of all five types of offshore drilling rigs. (Jennings Carnegie Public Library.)

With increasing distances and inaccessibility of offshore fields, floatplanes became important means of transportation in the Gulf of Mexico. Baroid utilized floatplanes to transport mud engineers to offshore platforms. Landing and taking off in the Gulf was a matter of timing the swells. Mistiming the swells could mean flying "downhill" when trying to take off or landing nose-first into a swell. Bill Egger apparently mistimed his distance to a drilling platform when he flew his airplane too close to a derrick leg and smacked the wing tip. (McNeese State University.)

Around 1937, Gulf Oil Corporation's amphibious marsh buggy drew inspiration from three sources: automobiles, tractors, and boats. This machine, which was the first of its kind, was built in Pittsburgh to help the Gulf Research and Development Company explore areas that were previously inaccessible. During the late 1930s, surveyors and prospectors of the Gulf Oil Company used the marsh buggy to scout new oilfields on the Louisiana coast. (Jennings Carnegie Public Library.)

Floating off into the sunset en route to its next drilling location, *Mr. Charlie* went on to drill more than 2.3 million feet of wells in the Gulf of Mexico. By the mid-1980s, offshore drilling activity had moved well past the 40-foot depth, leaving *Mr. Charlie* effectively unemployed. It gained new life through the preservation efforts of the International Petroleum Museum & Exposition, and on March 17, 2012, the American Society of Mechanical Engineers designated it a historic mechanical engineering landmark. (International Petroleum Museum & Exposition.)

Five

LIFE IN THE CAMPS AND CELEBRATING THE OIL INDUSTRY

An abundance of oilfield workers accompanied the oil booms throughout Louisiana. Some areas on the oilfields needed to be tended 24 hours a day, which required the help of many employees. At a time when the average wage in the United States was around $2.50 per day, an oilfield roustabout in the early 1900s could make $3 a day for a 10-hour shift. These workers moved into boomtowns or tent camps located within the oilfields.

Oil companies organized many of the camps on lands they leased for production. Some of the camps and boomtowns became raucous and rowdy places where the men had extra money on their hands, and the gambling and drinking establishments, often housed in tents themselves, were eager to take their earnings. Other camps were much more orderly where the men's families lived with them and tents housed schools for their children. In addition to new towns and camps that sprang up, existing towns that were near the oilfields became prosperous business centers and places of residence for landowners made rich from oil royalties and the multitude of oil companies vying to get the most out of the opportunities they saw in Louisiana.

Through the decades that the oil and gas industry has shaped the state's identity, Louisianans have recognized the importance of their petroleum culture and organized celebrations such as the Shrimp and Petroleum Festival in Morgan City, the Fur and Wildlife Festival in Cameron, and Gusher Days in Caddo Parish to celebrate their oil heritage.

Evangeline, in the Jennings Oilfield, was one of the first towns to develop because of the need for housing in the oil patch. Prior to the discovery of oil, the area that became Evangeline consisted of a couple of homes and buildings owned by the landowners who were farming in the area. It grew into a town with many inhabitants and the businesses to support them. (McNeese State University.)

Brothers John and Timothy Mooring were the namesakes of Mooringsport, where they started a ferry service across Caddo Lake. When the Kansas City Southern Railroad was planning its route to Shreveport in the 1880s, Mooringsport businessmen convinced them to come across the lake and through their town. The town was further transformed in the 1900s by the influx of oilfield workers and oil and gas production businesses. After drilling in Caddo Lake began, Gulf Oil Company located its offices in Mooringsport. This is a bird's-eye view of the "derrick city" in 1912. (Louisiana State Oil and Gas Museum.)

Oil City was a true boomtown amid the Caddo Oilfield. It was founded in 1903 as a stop along the Kansas City Southern Railroad. Prior to being named Oil City, this area consisted of three small towns named Ananias, Surrey, and Caddo City. By 1912, Oil City was the center of activity in the Caddo Oilfield. The city was notoriously rough and tumble, with roughnecks frequenting the saloons, gambling halls, and brothels. It was said that law enforcement tied drunks to the tree in the center of town until they were sober. (Louisiana State Oil and Gas Museum.)

Due to the competition among companies and the desire for oil, one of the oilfield jobs that was required around the clock was that of a well guard. These men protected this well in the Caddo Oilfield in 1918 with their shotguns in hand. Men also often armed themselves for protection against hijackers at the well sites. (Louisiana State Oil and Gas Museum.)

From left to right are Jeff Alexander, Mr. Pickle, Harry Smith, Shorty Burris, and Harry Nichols at the camp on the lakefront lease at Clear Lake near Oil City in 1914. The boiler station can be seen in the background. (Louisiana State Oil and Gas Museum.)

In the fast-growing oilfields of northwest Louisiana, many crews, and sometimes their families, lived in tent camps. This was the camp of the Gulf Pipeline Company in Caddo Oilfield in 1918. (Louisiana State Oil and Gas Museum.)

Even in the more established towns, like Oil City, many people lived in tent structures. Tents not only served as residences, they also housed schools, bars, restaurants, and many other businesses. In front of this tent house in Oil City in the early 1920s stand, from left to right, Belle the dog and Gordon, Myrta, and Mrs. Hal Boylston. (Louisiana State Oil and Gas Museum.)

After unsuccessful attempts to control their employees with the aid of a Texas Ranger, Mike Benedum and Joe Trees of the Trees Oil Company decided to build a proper camp for their employees, which became Trees City, Louisiana. The men believed that their employees would be more efficient if they had comfortable places to sleep, good food, and places to recreate. The structures in this view of Trees City look much more permanent than those in other oilfield camp photographs. (Both, Louisiana State Oil and Gas Museum.)

Trees City was the camp town established in response to disorderly towns like Oil City and Vivian. But even in Trees City, the oilfield workers wound down at the end of the day drinking a beer and shooting pool in the pool hall in 1916. (Louisiana State Oil and Gas Museum.)

Trees City was more prepared for family life than many other oilfield camps. Children and wives of oil workers enjoyed this playground in Trees City in 1918. Oil derricks can be seen in the background across the horizon. (Louisiana State Oil and Gas Museum.)

Oilfield workers entertained themselves in the Gulf Pipeline Company Camp in Caddo Oilfield in 1917 with card games. The entertainment tent was the main place for the workers to spend their leisure time, since many of the camps were far removed from the nearest towns. (Louisiana State Oil and Gas Museum.)

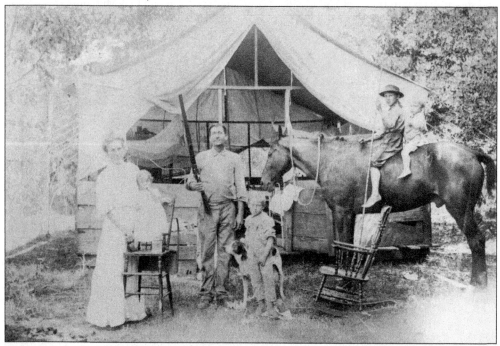

Due to the lack of established housing in the oilfields, families joined the men in tent houses. This tent, with wooden floors and walls, would have had more privacy and protection from wild creatures than a typical canvas tent. Graham's camp housed this family of six. (Louisiana State Oil and Gas Museum.)

An oilfield family poses for a photograph on top of a steam boiler. Massive boilers like this one powered steam engines used for drilling and pumping oil wells. They also came in handy when putting out well fires. (Louisiana State Oil and Gas Museum.)

In 1920, after successfully bringing in a well, driller J.N. Darnell and his crew celebrated with a beer or two in the Caddo Oilfield. (Louisiana State Oil and Gas Museum.)

This large oilfield camp tent provided several "rooms" in which workers could have a small bit of privacy from communal living. Workers shared everything in the camps, including the "tobacco" crate, written with three men's names, and a game of cards. (Louisiana State Oil and Gas Museum.)

A roughneck rides the derrick elevator in the Caddo Oilfield in 1920. The elevator was used to lift or lower the drill pipe or casing by attaching it to the fitting on the end of the elevator. (Louisiana State Oil and Gas Museum.)

By the 1920s, Oil City was an established boomtown, and as such, buildings that were more permanent were constructed, including the Young Men's Christian Association Building. The YMCA would have provided a healthy recreational outlet for the men working and living in crowded conditions. (Louisiana State Oil and Gas Museum.)

If one looks closely, one can see the oilfield workers from the Jack Darnell drilling crew literally hanging out on the oil derrick in Oil City, Louisiana, in 1926. (Louisiana State Oil and Gas Museum.)

The Daniel family gather around the Bosticle well that Tom Bell drilled in Vivian, Louisiana. From left to right, Leland, Louise, Marshall, unidentified, Madge, and children Earleen, Tommy, and Jack visited the well in the 1930s. (Louisiana State University, Shreveport.)

The "Texaco Beauties," representing each oilfield area in the vicinity, pose at the Texaco Camp on Cross Lake near Shreveport, Louisiana, around 1947. Judges did not crown a winner. From left to right, the contestants are ? Strahan, O.B. Brown, R.F. Burks, Reese Gullet, Homer Crum, ? Collins, ? Dooley, and ? Baker. (Louisiana State Oil and Gas Museum.)

Jennings celebrated the 50th anniversary of the discovery of oil with the Golden Oil Jubilee in 1951. The parade through downtown had 33 floats honoring the oil industry and the benefits it brought to Louisiana. This view of the parade shows that the town was decorated festively for the event, and many people were in attendance, even though it rained on their parade. (Jennings Carnegie Public Library.)

Jennings Oil Company sponsored this float with a replica of the first oil well derrick in the Jennings Oilfield, well No. 1, September 21, 1901. Two parade queens rode on the float in celebration. (Jennings Carnegie Public Library.)

The Gulf Oil float commemorated the many uses of oil and gas products. The float included a gasoline pump for vehicles, along with a gas station attendant and a barrel of oil that was typically used by farmers. (Jennings Carnegie Public Library.)

Most of the oil companies participated in the parade, including Stanolind Oil and Gas Company, which sponsored multiple floats. This one displayed its field operations, including a "Christmas tree" of valves, spools, and fittings, and a man lying on a cot wearing his PPE (Personal Protective Equipment) gas mask. (Jennings Carnegie Public Library.)

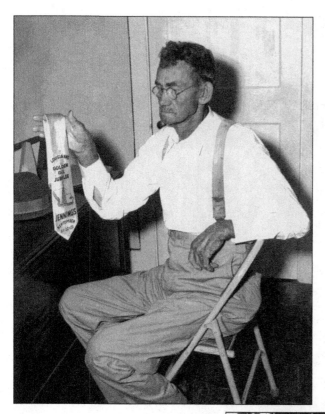

Bob Hines shows off the ties produced for the jubilee. In 1951, Hines was a 79-year-old veteran of the Louisiana oilfields. He traveled to Jennings in 1951 to join the Old Timers Club at the Golden Oil Jubilee. In 1903, he started working for the Crowley Oil & Mineral Co. He started as a roustabout, next became a driller, and then was a stockholder in the firm. He later drilled the first well in the Vinton Field, hiring himself and his rig out for $500 a month. (Jennings Carnegie Public Library.)

The jubilee gave special recognition to those who had been working in the oil and gas industry for longer lengths of time. V.J. "Pop" Guidry proudly wore his commemorative Old Timer ribbon. The 70-year-old man held a five-month-old child, and a newspaper article stated they were possibly the youngest and oldest people in attendance. Guidry lived in Jennings in 1900, and by 1951, he had retired from his oilfield work as a roughneck and roustabout. (Jennings Carnegie Public Library.)

Bumper sticker souvenirs advertised the Golden Oil Jubilee in Jennings in 1951. In order to plan the Golden Oil Jubilee, 33 members of the oil and gas industry served as members of the advisory committee. The celebration started with the dedication ceremony on Friday, September 21, 1951, followed by three days of events including handicraft demonstrations, tours of plants and yards, musical entertainment, a parade, boat races, an air show, a fashion show, fireworks, and square dancing. (Jennings Carnegie Public Library.)

R.H. "Joe" Lewis served as the caller of the square dance at the Golden Oil Jubilee. The square dance was held on the first day of the Jubilee on Friday, September 21, following the fireworks show over Lake Arthur. (Jennings Carnegie Public Library.)

Festive square dancers donned skirts with the Esso emblem at the Golden Oil Jubilee. The following night, another dance was held called the "Roughneck's Ball." Tex Beneke and his orchestra entertained the dancers for hours. (Jennings Carnegie Public Library.)

From left to right are Mrs. W. Scott Heywood, B.A. Hardey of Shreveport, and W.A. "Stud" Grapes, the second vice president of the Golden Oil Jubilee, who unveiled the new exhibit dedicated to the first oil well in Louisiana. The exhibit included a replica oil derrick and boiler along with informative signage. It is still located at the Louisiana Oil and Gas Park in Jennings, Louisiana. (Jennings Carnegie Public Library.)

Mrs. W. Scott Heywood poses by the sign commemorating the first oil well in Louisiana drilled by her late husband. Much of the funding for the Golden Oil Jubilee came from the oil companies that operated in the area. W.T. Burton, a prominent Lake Charles oilman at the time, was the first to contribute to the fund. Thanks to the generous contributions, no admissions were charged for any events in connection with the jubilee. (Jennings Carnegie Public Library.)

Many people attended the dedication ceremony for the replica of the first oil well, as seen in this overall view of the event. The dedication ceremony was the kickoff event to the Golden Oil Jubilee on September 21, 1951, fifty years to the day of the first successful oil well in Louisiana. (Jennings Carnegie Public Library.)

More than 50 years after the discovery of oil on the Jules Clement property northeast of Jennings, Mrs. Jules Clement, who was 93 years old in 1951, was still receiving royalty checks. The Jennings-Heywood Oil Syndicate had been leasing that property, where the first oil well in Louisiana was drilled, and Mrs. W. Scott Heywood, its president, presented Mrs. Clement with her check. (Jennings Carnegie Public Library.)

As part of the Golden Oil Jubilee, an exhibit hall held displays from various oil companies and companies that depended on the oil industry. This exhibit from the Ohio Oil Company displays a replica derrick and photograph of the Cotton Valley Operators Recycling Committee Recycling Plant in Cotton Valley, Louisiana. The oil recycling plant, in northwestern Louisiana, was built in 1941 at a cost of $2.25 million. (Jennings Carnegie Public Library.)

The Pan-Am exhibit showed many of the products created from petroleum. Some of the products in the display included Camel Vulcanizing Patch Units, Permalube Motor Oil, Pan-Am Fan Belts, Valvoline, antifreeze, gasoline, brake fluid, and tires. (Jennings Carnegie Public Library.)

The Esso display focused on how the farmer, in his day-to-day activities, utilized Esso products. This was, and still is, very applicable to most of Louisiana where farming and oil and gas production coexist. Products like tractor fuel, grease, asphalt, insecticides, waxes, and weed killer were used by many in the farming industry. (Jennings Carnegie Public Library.)

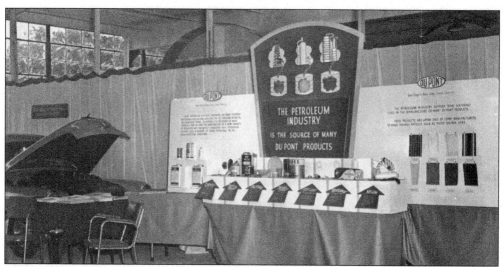

The DuPont exhibit illustrated that the petroleum industry was the source of many DuPont products. The sign stated that crude petroleum was the source of many chemicals that went into the manufacturing of a wide variety of products not ordinarily associated with petroleum. Some projects in their display included Lucite, Teflon, and Nylon. (Jennings Carnegie Public Library.)

The Sunray Oils exhibit included a graphic of the process of "Petroleum from the Ground to You," along with chemistry equipment used in the processing of petroleum products. The sign above the booth reads, "Your Progress and Oil Progress go Hand in Hand." Esso used this same graphic in an advertisement welcoming all of the members of the industry to Louisiana's Golden Oil Jubilee. (Jennings Carnegie Public Library.)

Each year in Cameron Parish, the Fur and Wildlife Festival recognizes one of the industries that has shaped the parish, including the petroleum industry. Approximately every five years, the festival celebrates the importance of the petroleum industry to the parish. The program cover from the 16th Annual Fur and Wildlife Festival in 1972 appears at right. The program, below, included many articles about the oil industry and its heritage in Cameron Parish. (Both, McNeese State University.)

Visit us at
arcadiapublishing.com

CPSIA information can be obtained
at www.ICGtesting.com
Printed in the USA
LVOW02*0724270617

539400LV00045B/1637/P

9 781531 663759